Seven B[ays]

in

Seven Days

South Devon

Creating unforgettable days in South Devon

Jan White

Published by: Drifting Sand Publishing, 21 Southey Crescent, Kingskerswell, Devon TQ12 5JQ driftingsandpublishing@gmail.com

A CIP record of this book is available from the British Library.

First published 2018

Printed and bound by Newton Print, Newton Abbot, Devon

ISBN 978-1-5272-2574-9

Recipe for Contented Children

Ingredients

A sandy beach
Rock pools (optional)
Bucket
One or two dogs
Pebbles, shells and driftwood
Stretch of cool, gentle waves

Method

Combine children and dogs, blending till fully infused.
Work in sand between toes and paws.
Decorate sand with pebbles, shells and driftwood arranging in patterns.
Saturate the blue of the sky and green of the sea with sunny warmth till all are rosy and fully marinated.
Gently cool down and chill at the water's edge.
Remove contented children, still smiling, and dogs to rest area.

Jan White

John

With all my love

Contents

Did you know?

There are 89.8 miles or 144.5 km of coastline to explore between Wembury and Exmouth. That should be enough coast to keep us all going for a while.......

Wembury Beach

Parking – 2 car parks; one along from the Marine Centre (Two Moors Way) at Wembury Beach. PL9 0HP – National Trust car parking charges apply (free to NT members) and Wembury Point car park at PL9 0BA (Donations); some limited free road parking

Type of beach and access – Mainly sand with some areas of shingle and rocks with good access

Cafes – The Old Mill Cafe on the beach serves breakfast. lunch. afternoon cream teas

Toilets – On the beach. opposite cafe

Lifeguards – None present so children will need to be supervised

Dogs allowed – Out of season dogs are allowed on parts of the beach but the coastal paths allow access all year round.

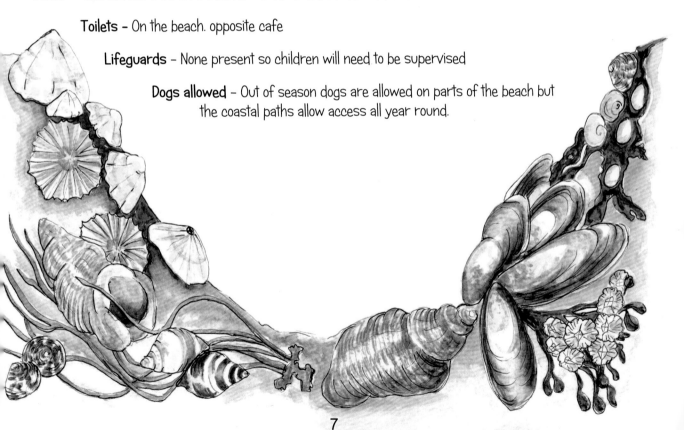

Stunning views of the Mewstone Rock can be seen from the beach. Now a sanctuary inhabited by sea birds, including cormorants and shags, it is interesting to note that in it's past the Mewstone has been a private residence; a prison; and a smuggler's refuge! With binoculars the remains of the building, once a home, can be seen.

Wembury Church – The Saxon wooden church was replaced by the existing building in 1088 by the Normans (main part) and further extensive work carried out in the 1880's. The church is dedicated to St Werburgh's and a stained glass window dedicated to him was made in 1886.

Wembury Marine Centre, on the edge of the beach, is at the centre of the Wembury Voluntary Marine Conservation Area, and offers a range of interactive ways to learn about local wildlife and conservation.

The Old Mill Cafe serves breakfast, teas and light snacks and literally sits on the beach!

Leisurely Walk (about 1.9 miles)

Start at either Wembury beach or Wembury Point car park. From the beach car park head to the beach, going over the slipway with the cafe on your left. Pick up the coastal path running parallel to the beach. Follow the path for about 10/15 minutes when you reach a gated entrance to a slipway leading to the old Lido and boathouse. Continue west along the coast path and walk through another gate which will take you uphill on a steeper path. A further small gate lets you pass an old military stone marker with 'No10' and a picture of an anchor on it. From here you will see the houses of Heybrook Bay. Take a very sharp turn right at the first white house, signed with a SW coast marker, and follow the path forward, past the National Trust sign 'Wembury Point & Mewstone' and, walking through a gate, continue on the path through to a tarmac drive. Don't go through, but keep right of the next gate, continuing through as the road widens. A grass path will bring you back to the slipway and old boathouse. Bear left and complete the walk back retracing your steps.

From Wembury Point car park – Go through the gate at the car park, and follow the road to the next gate. Go through this, make a sharp turn left and continue. As the path turns to grass bear right towards the beach and continue the walk (as above) from the slipway leading to the old Lido and boathouse. On the return part of the walk follow the path up the tarmac drive towards the left through the gate back to car park at Wembury Point.

(Not to scale)

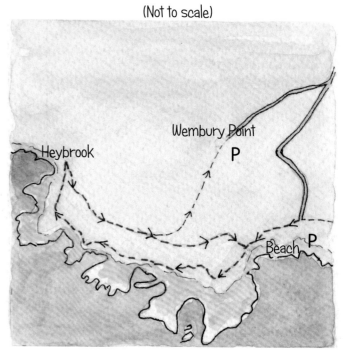

10

Just behind the Coastal Path sign on the beach lay a colourful range of surfing and kayaking equipment and rafts, glinting in the sunshine, waiting eagerly to be taken out to sea!

Sloe or Blackthorn

Elder, hawthorn and sloe trees live happily together along the coastal path, displaying an abundance of white blossom in spring followed by enticing colourful berries later in the season.......

Hawthorn or May Tree

Elder

The National Trust omegas are a familiar sight to walkers and indeed form a familiar part of the landscape........

THE NATIONAL TRUST

WEMBURY POINT & GREAT MEWSTONE

Common reed forms dense clumps along the path

Overlooking the sea a dedicated bench keeps memories alive......

Blackberries juicy and ripe. ready for picking!

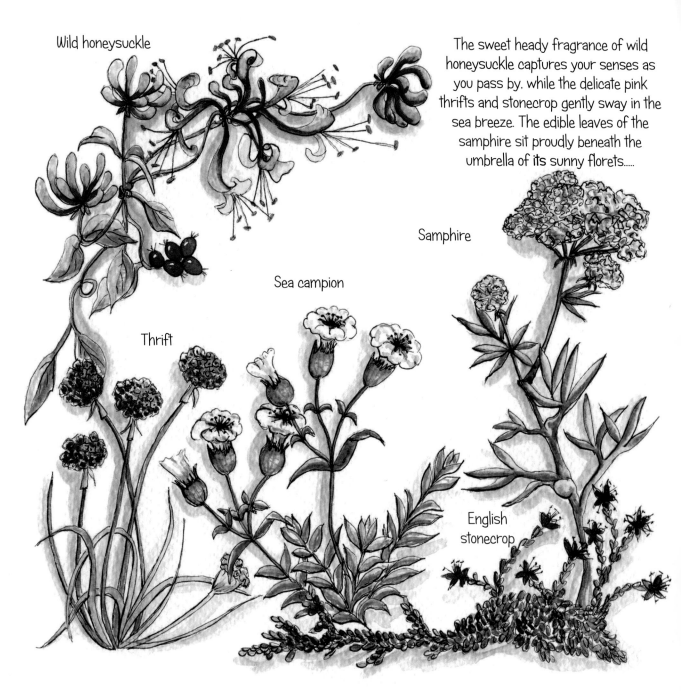

Wild honeysuckle

The sweet heady fragrance of wild honeysuckle captures your senses as you pass by. while the delicate pink thrifts and stonecrop gently sway in the sea breeze. The edible leaves of the samphire sit proudly beneath the umbrella of its sunny florets......

Samphire

Sea campion

Thrift

English stonecrop

Residents of the Mewstone Rock bird sanctuary, these shags are on look out patrol!

Picnic Lunch
Asparagus Frittata

Ingredients – serves 4
165g small new potatoes
150g asparagus tips
90g fresh or frozen peas
2 medium courgette, chopped
bunch of spring onions, diced
glug of olive oil
6 large eggs
1 tbsp fresh tarragon or chervil
seasoning

Method

Simmer the potatoes for 10/15 minutes until just cooked and drain. Cut the asparagus into small lengths and cook for 2/3 minutes with the peas. Gently saute the courgettes and spring onions until just soft in a large frying pan. Lower the hob to a very gentle heat. Add the asparagus, peas and potatoes. Beat the eggs, herbs and seasoning and pour over the vegetables. The eggs need to cook slowly so cover the pan and leave for about 10/12 minutes until almost set. Finish off cooking the eggs under the grill.

Serve with a simple green salad.

Wembury Marine Centre is run by Devon Wildlife Trust, as part of the Wembury Marine Centre partnership.

The Centre, which is completely free to visit, was built in 1994 and refurbished in 2006. Inside is filled with a array of resources including interactive displays, marine tanks, and fun games. They also offer amazing Rockpool Rambles and other events to help find and identify a range of marine life living in the sheltered slate reefs in this Voluntary Marine Conservation Area. You can also learn about the importance of conservation as the area nearby is designated a Special Area of Conservation. You'll be amazed at what you can find out!

It is open from April to September.

Devon Wildlife Trust's Wembury Marine Centre Seashore Code

Leave your fishing nets at home, and follow the Seashore Code
using your hands and buckets to catch the creatures.

Put Me Back!
Always replace animals, rocks and
seaweed where
you found them. Don't leave
animals in buckets

Don't make me homeless!
Only collect empty shells.

I don't like litter!
Take your rubbish home – litter is a killer
for the wildlife

Handle me with care
Poking or squeezing soft bodied
animals like sea anemones can harm
them. Don't use a net to catch rock
pool creatures.

Look after yourself!
Wembury is a wonderful place but
be careful, the rocks can be
slippery, the cliffs can be high and
the tides change quickly

Hey! I'm down here!
Watch where you walk, you can easily dislodge
or crush small sea creatures

Starfish

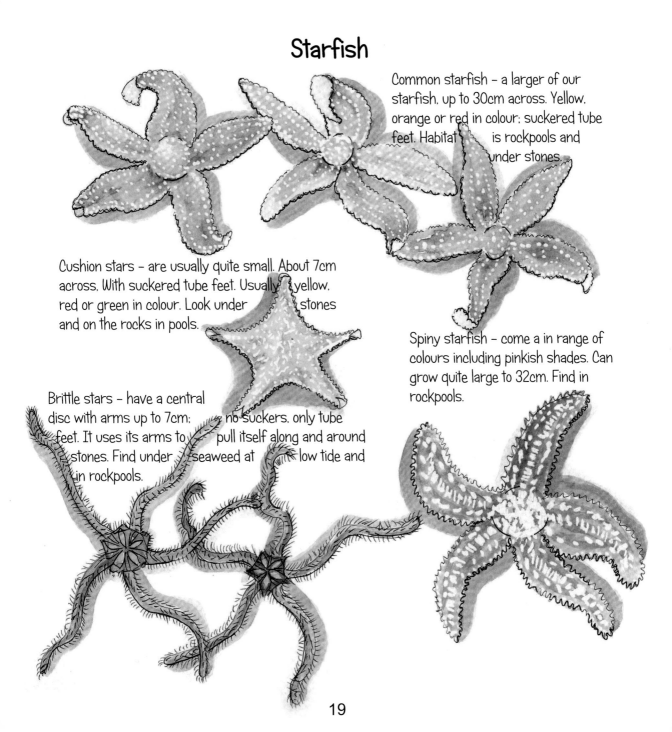

Common starfish - a larger of our starfish, up to 30cm across. Yellow, orange or red in colour; suckered tube feet. Habitat   is rockpools and   under stones.

Cushion stars - are usually quite small. About 7cm across. With suckered tube feet. Usually   yellow, red or green in colour. Look under   stones and on the rocks in pools.

Spiny starfish - come a in range of colours including pinkish shades. Can grow quite large to 32cm. Find in rockpools.

Brittle stars - have a central disc with arms up to 7cm;   no suckers, only tube feet. It uses its arms to   pull itself along and around stones. Find under   seaweed at   low tide and in rockpools.

Rockpool Fish

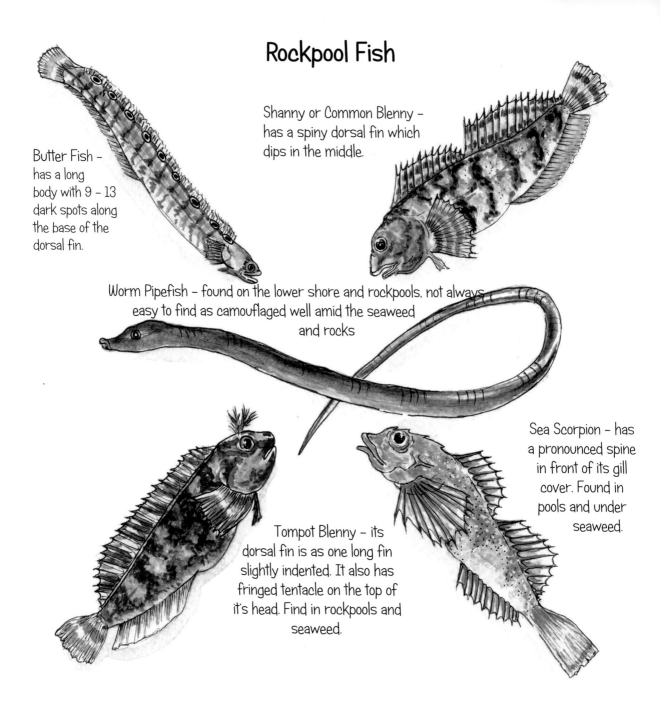

Butter Fish – has a long body with 9 – 13 dark spots along the base of the dorsal fin.

Shanny or Common Blenny – has a spiny dorsal fin which dips in the middle.

Worm Pipefish – found on the lower shore and rockpools, not always easy to find as camouflaged well amid the seaweed and rocks

Tompot Blenny – its dorsal fin is as one long fin slightly indented. It also has fringed tentacle on the top of it's head. Find in rockpools and seaweed.

Sea Scorpion – has a pronounced spine in front of its gill cover. Found in pools and under seaweed.

Crabs

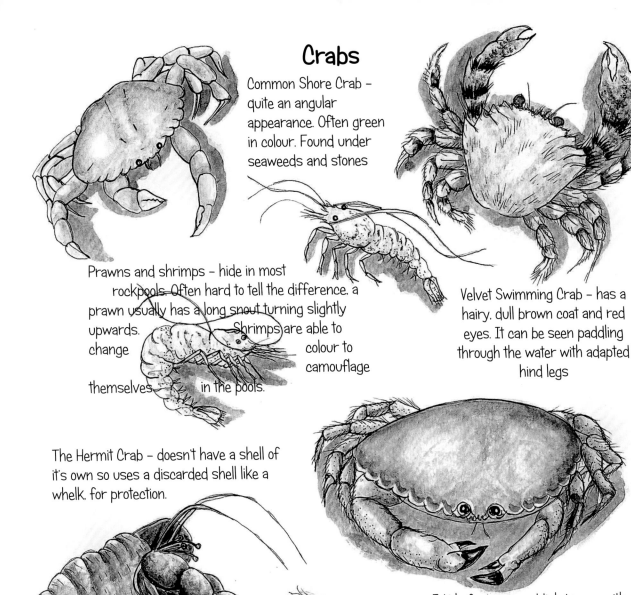

Common Shore Crab – quite an angular appearance. Often green in colour. Found under seaweeds and stones

Prawns and shrimps – hide in most rockpools. Often hard to tell the difference. a prawn usually has a long snout turning slightly upwards. Shrimps are able to change colour to camouflage themselves in the pools.

Velvet Swimming Crab – has a hairy. dull brown coat and red eyes. It can be seen paddling through the water with adapted hind legs

The Hermit Crab – doesn't have a shell of it's own so uses a discarded shell like a whelk. for protection.

Edible Crab – is reddish brown with black tipped claws. It has a pie crust edge to it's shell and is easily found on rocky shores

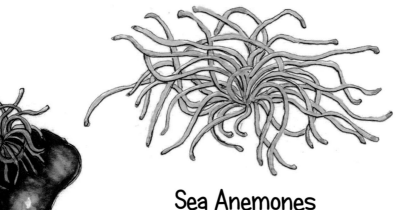

Sea Anemones

The Beadlet anemone – with its dark red jelly like body, and the Strawberry Anemone – looking like its name are most common on the shore. Found in rockpools they can be seen with their feeding fringe tentacles out ready to capture passing prey if the pool is filled with water. If exposed to air when the tide is low, it simply withdraws its fringe to save water loss until the tide comes back in!

The Snakelocks Anemone – adorns beautiful colours of green with purple ended tentacles and doesn't often retract its tentacles so has to ensure it stays in rockpools which never completely empty.

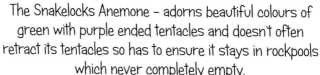

Making a Quill Pen

You will need
a large wing feather, about 20 cm long, seagull
feathers are perfect
tweezers
marker pen
a craft or sharp knife
cutting board
non permanent ink

How to make
        As you want the writing point of your pen to go
downwards towards your paper, look at your feather and find
the natural 'curve' it takes. Use the marker to make a mark
where you want the writing point to be. Cut the quill, on the
cutting board, from the point you've marked on a slant at 45%
with a sharp knife. Use the tweezers to clean out any debris
from shaft before dipping your pen in ink and displaying your
writing skills!

Did you know?

The Magna
Carta was
signed in 1215
with a quill pen,
and the word
pen comes
from the Latin
word Penna
which means
pen!

Pan fried scallops with smoked bacon and spinach

Created by Nick & Anita Hutchings, Britannia @The Beach Beesands, Kingsbridge

Ingredients – serves 2
a thick slice of fresh crusty bread
knob of unsalted butter
splash of olive oil
100g smoked bacon, chopped
6–8 hand-dived scallops
50g spinach leaves, washed.

Method
Cut the slice of bread in half and set aside. Add the butter, a splash of oil and the chopped bacon to a hot pan. Cook on a medium heat for around 2 minutes (be careful not to burn the butter). Turn up the heat and add the scallops to the pan, searing them for around 1 minute on each side. When the bacon starts to crisp up, add the spinach and let it wilt, tossing it gently with the bacon and scallops.

To serve
Place four scallops on each piece of bread; this will soak up all those lovely cooking juices. Add the bacon and spinach mixture to the plate and enjoy!

Slapton Sands

Parking – Memorial car park next to the beach.TQ7 2EA Torcross and Strete Gate. pay and display: Slapton Bridge – free limited parking.

Type of beach and access – Pebble and shingle beach stretching 3 miles. level access to beach from Memorial car park

Cafes – Shops pubs etc. in Slapton and Torcross;

Toilets – at the Memorial car park. Torcross and Strete Gate

Lifeguards – From July – September. check RNLI website for details

Dogs allowed – Yes. all year

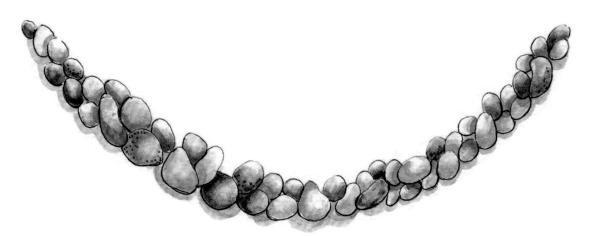

Rounding the final bend to the bay, Slapton Sands greets with its wide welcome, a vast expanse of cool blue water, and 3 miles of beach inviting every visitor........

The Monument in the car park adjacent to the turn off for Slapton commemorates the sacrifice made by 750 families from surrounding local villages who, in 1943, were given short notice to pack everything, including livestock, and vacate the area which was requisitioned as a practice area for the D-day manoeuvres.

The long narrow beach of Slapton Sands reaches over to Torcross and it's here that this unusual piece of military equipment stands as a reminder..........

This American Sherman tank took part in the D - Day practice landings at Slapton beach in 1944 where it was lost at sea and there remained until it's recovery in 1984.
It stands as a memorial to those American lives lost during the course of the D - Day practice landings at Slapton beach in 1944. Their sacrifice was not in vain. Be they ever at peace.

The beach seems to go on forever, the crunch of the shingle below, the only distraction, with the gentle ebb and flow of the tide interjected by occasional noisy sea birds. Easy to lose yourself in total relaxation............

Some plants have adapted to a life which can be harsh and these flowers are among some which grow on the edge of the beach and Ley. able to cope with salt from the sea. at times strong winds and often with little fresh water. They look stunning!

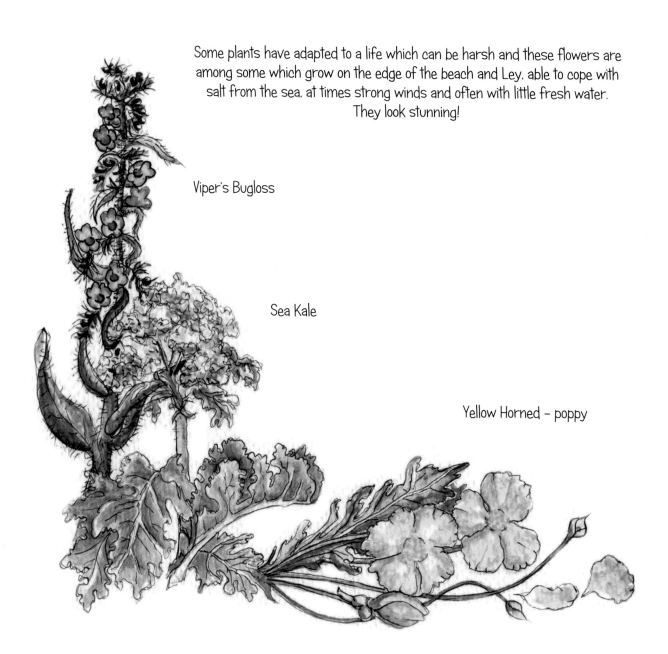

Viper's Bugloss

Sea Kale

Yellow Horned – poppy

Picnic Lunch
Aubergine Dip

Ingredients –serves 4

2 large aubergines
2 garlic cloves, crushed
juice of 1 ½ lemons
¼ teasp smoked paprika
2 tbsp chopped fresh mint or parsley
2 tbsp virgin olive oil
handful of black olives
pita breads or crackers to serve

Method

Heat the oven to 375 F, 190C, gas mark 5. Prick the aubergines all over and place on a baking sheet in the oven for 20/30 minutes. When the skins of the aubergines are blackened and softened, almost collapsing, bring them out and leave on one side to cool down. When room temperature, remove and discard the skins, then mash the flesh with a fork in a bowl. Add the garlic, lemon juice, smoked paprika and half the mint or parsley. Pile into a sealed food container or serving dish, and gently drizzle over the olive oil. Finally top with the olives, and sprinkle over the remaining chopped herbs.

Serve with pita breads or crackers.

Leisurely Walk (about 1.75 miles)

From the main road (A379) Memorial car park turn right and walk up the road, crossing at the signpost for Slapton Village. Go over Slapton Bridge where there's an easily accessible viewing platform, and continue up the road. Further up on the right is the Slapton Ley Field Centre offering free events, a range of courses as well as educational visits, easy to use guides for purchase to identify local wildlife and information on the valuable work carried out by the centre. Continue to follow the road round passing the Slapton Village shop and Gospel Hall on your left. As the road ascends take a turning on the left signposted with a public footpath sign. You will pass through a gate as the path narrows and will see polytunnels on your left.

Continue your walk passing through wet woodland, walking on boardwalks and taking advantage of the numerous benches and viewing platforms available to enhance your experience. The Hazel coppice is awash with colour from Spring onwards and the Ireland bird hide is perfect for quiet viewing. As you make your way round the edge of the Ley, the walk ends on Slapton Bridge, close to car parks.

(Not to scale)

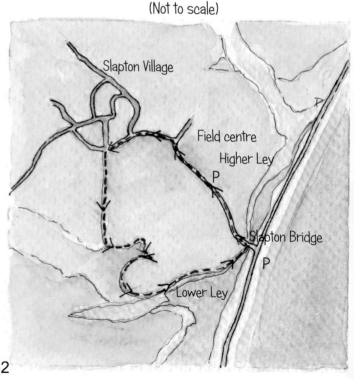

Slapton Village

Field centre
Higher Ley
P

Slapton Bridge
P

Lower Ley

Village signposts lead the way.....

The village shop

A recessed bench tucked into a wall of greenery along the way allows for an impromptu rest........

There are plenty of signs along the road and lanes to the village

Beautiful stonework creates amazing circular gate posts and the paths take your vision far and beyond......

Around the Ley...

The Coot is 36 – 38cm in length and is from the bird family of coots, rails and crakes. It has a silky black plumage with a distinctive white beak and frontal shield. Their lobed feet allow them to dive and swim precisely in the same manner as webbed feet.

The Great Crested Grebe is 46 – 51cm long and from the bird family of grebes. It is a very dignified bird with impressive raised head feathers. They dive to feed and can move long distances under water. Young grebes are often seen riding on their parents' backs.

The Tufted Duck is 40 – 47cm and from the bird family of swans, geese and ducks The male's plumage is a striking black and white with a long often drooping crest.

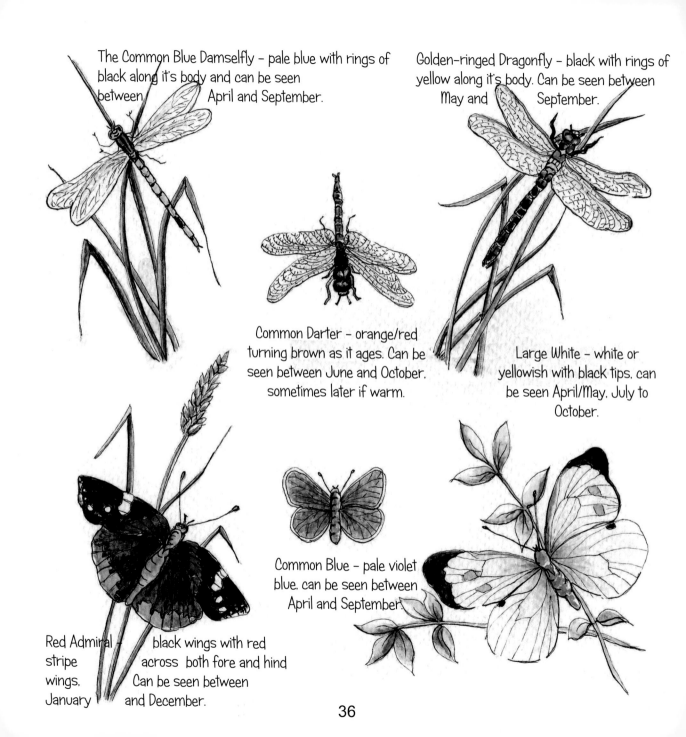

The Common Blue Damselfly - pale blue with rings of black along it's body and can be seen between April and September.

Golden-ringed Dragonfly - black with rings of yellow along it's body. Can be seen between May and September.

Common Darter - orange/red turning brown as it ages. Can be seen between June and October. sometimes later if warm.

Large White - white or yellowish with black tips. can be seen April/May. July to October.

Red Admiral - black wings with red stripe across both fore and hind wings. Can be seen between January and December.

Common Blue - pale violet blue. can be seen between April and September.

36

I was very excited to find such an array of hides, look outs and benches in which to observe the vast number of birds, insects and plants on, in and around Slapton Ley. My sketch book came out immediately I entered Ireland Bay Hide.....the perfect location!

Listen out for the Cetti's Warbler, their song is in loud bursts

A Coastal Sketch Book to Record your Finds

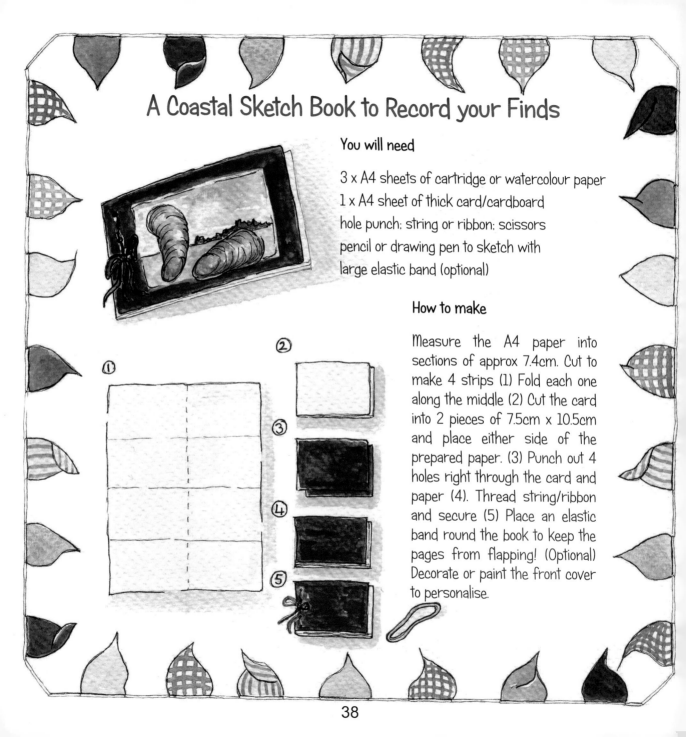

You will need

3 x A4 sheets of cartridge or watercolour paper
1 x A4 sheet of thick card/cardboard
hole punch; string or ribbon; scissors
pencil or drawing pen to sketch with
large elastic band (optional)

How to make

Measure the A4 paper into sections of approx 7.4cm. Cut to make 4 strips (1) Fold each one along the middle (2) Cut the card into 2 pieces of 7.5cm x 10.5cm and place either side of the prepared paper. (3) Punch out 4 holes right through the card and paper (4). Thread string/ribbon and secure (5) Place an elastic band round the book to keep the pages from flapping! (Optional) Decorate or paint the front cover to personalise.

Thai fish cakes with Thai cucumber sauce

Created by the South Devon Chilli Farm, Loddiswell, Kingsbridge

Ingredients – Fish cakes – Serves 2

225g raw skinless whiting fillet, flaked
1 onion, finely chopped
1 stick lemon grass, finely chopped
1 tbsp fresh parsley, finely chopped
1 hot fresh chilli such as Ring of Fire, Serrano or Aji Limon, chopped (or use dried Piri Piri or de Arbol if out of season)
1 tbsp fish sauce; 1 egg; 2 tbsp corn flour
pinch of sugar
oil for frying

Sauce

½ cucumber, peeled and sliced thinly
50g sugar; 250 ml boiling water
120 ml wine vinegar; 1 tsp salt
2 shallots, finely chopped
2 fresh red chillies, finely chopped (hot chilli) Use less if you don't want too much heat....

Preparation – Fish cakes

Mix all ingredients together either by hand or in a food processor. Form into small fish cakes. Shallow or deep fry for about 10 mins until golden and cooked through. Drain and serve with the cucumber sauce and a side salad.

Sauce

Arrange the cucumber slices in a bowl. Dissolve the sugar in the water. Mix in the wine vinegar, salt, shallots and chillies. Pour over the cucumber, cover and chill until needed.

www.southdevonchillifarm.co.uk

Brixham - Fishcombe Cove

Parking – Brixham central car park Middle Street TQ5 8DY up to 3 hours, pay and display; Breakwater car park TQ5 9AF long stay, pay and display; Freshwater car park TQ5 8BA long stay, pay and display.

Type of beach and access – a beautiful shingle and sandy cove, accessed via steps or steep path, care needs to be taken when accessing

Cafes – Fishcombe Cove beach cafe, a bright cafe offering a range of drinks, ices and snacks.

Toilets – at the top of the beach, no disabled or baby changing facilities. More toilets in Brixham harbour including disabled access.

Lifeguards – None present so children will need to be supervised

Dogs allowed – Yes, all year round

I could spend hours day dreaming while watching the fishing boats coming and going in the busy harbour – the visitor viewing platform is the perfect place to watch from........The brightly coloured houses tumbling down the sides of the harbour bring additional vibrancy to the landscape!

Capstans have incredible strength and ability to provide a safe and secure mooring for fishing vessels ensuring safety in the harbour

At the end of the half mile Victoria breakwater a 9 metre high cast iron lighthouse stands. a glistening painted white. effective tower protecting the harbour. A lovely stroll lets you absorb the surroundings.........

43

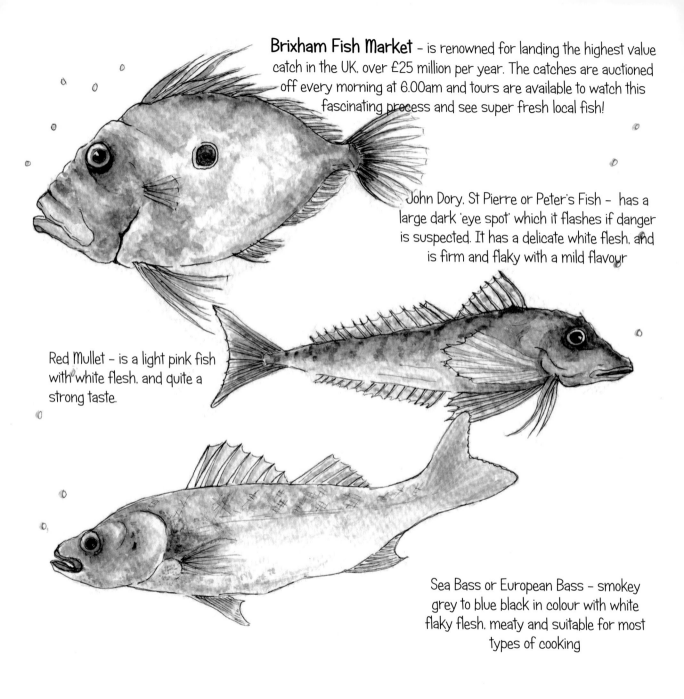

Brixham Fish Market - is renowned for landing the highest value catch in the UK. over £25 million per year. The catches are auctioned off every morning at 6.00am and tours are available to watch this fascinating process and see super fresh local fish!

John Dory. St Pierre or Peter's Fish - has a large dark 'eye spot' which it flashes if danger is suspected. It has a delicate white flesh. and is firm and flaky with a mild flavour

Red Mullet - is a light pink fish with white flesh. and quite a strong taste.

Sea Bass or European Bass - smokey grey to blue black in colour with white flaky flesh. meaty and suitable for most types of cooking

Plaice - is a right-eyed flounder, a scaleless flatfish. They are dark green to brown skinned fish, spotted with orange and have a sweet and mild flavour

Turbot - a large left eyed flatfish with a scaleless skin of brown with black spots and brown speckles. It has firm white flesh with a delicate flavour.

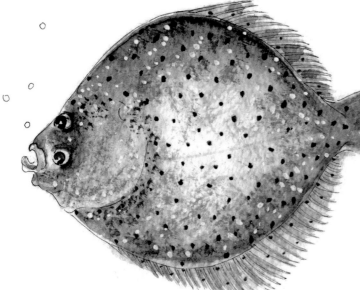

Lemon Sole - a right eyed scaleless skin flat fish. Its skin is a mottled reddish brown with flecks of pink, orange and yellow. It has a delicate sweet white flesh.

It seems these lobster pots may have been left unsupervised..........

A great escape indeed!

Mussels cling to the rocks waiting for the next tide to come in.....

Picnic Lunch

Mackerel pasta salad

Ingredients – serves 4

1 onion, finely chopped

1 x 400g tin chopped tomatoes

1 red pepper cut into chunks

2 x 120g tins mackerel in hot chilli sauce

1 x 400g tin berlotti beans

1 x 400g tin flagelet beans

280g pasta twists

grated cheese

Method

Boil the pasta according to packet instructions. Fry the onion until soft and then add the tomatoes, beans and mackerel to the pan. Stir and cook through for 10 minutes. Drain the pasta and mix with the mackerel and other ingredients. Allow to cool and season before placing in a sealed food container. Sprinkle with the grated cheese.

Leisurely Walk (about 1.6 miles)

Make your way to the harbour and follow the promenade flanking it till you reach the New Fish Quay and Brixham Fish Markets. Follow signs to Fishcombe Cove. The coastal path will bring you to Battery Gardens, where ample seating is provided to allow you to sit and enjoy the stunning views out to sea. There are a number of paths within the gardens to meander and enjoy. Continue along the main path to either the set of steps which lead down to the delightful Fishcombe Cove or continue a little further on and join a path down to Fishcombe Cove (this is quite steep). A cafe and toilets are located here. When you are ready to leave the cove, exit via the path straight ahead which leads to the Brixham Battery.

The Battery is well worth a visit as volunteers have restored and help to maintain the grounds including the A.T.S building, Generator Rooms, Ammunition Tunnels, Gun Emplacements, War Shelter, Battery Observation Post (B.O.P), Pill Box and other structures around the site. Admission is free with donations appreciated. From the Brixham Battery you can return through the gardens and retrace your steps along the coastal path to the harbour.

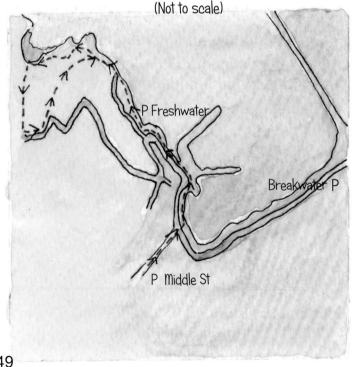

(Not to scale)

P Freshwater

Breakwater P

P Middle St

49

Fishcombe Cove Cafe – brightly painted and inviting!

FISHCOMBE COVE CAFE

SOUTH WEST COAST PATH
BRIXHAM HARBOUR

SOUTH WEST COAST PATH
PAIGNTON & BROADSANDS

The steps from the coastal path lead through this tunnel emerging on the sandy cove

FISHCOMBE COVE
BEACH CAFE
OPEN 10am till 4pm
SERVING HOT & COLD
FOOD & DRINKS
DECKING AREA
SEATING AVAILABLE
PANORAMIC VIEWS
ACROSS THE BAY.

Plenty of signposts to guide you and keep you on the right track!

50

Breathtaking views out from the cove.......

Fishcombe Eco - Mooring

This seagrass friendly eco mooring was initiated by local partners, to avoid boat anchoring activities damaging the seagrass beds, which are vulnerable to these pressures, by helping to keep disturbance off the sea bed. Seagrass improves the quality of water, and stores atmospheric carbon, essential to the environment. Acting as a safe management option for habitat the mooring will still enable boat owners to fully enjoy the beautiful cove with minimal disruption to these vital grasses. The mooring can be clearly seen from the cove.

Sand Gaper

Queen Scallop

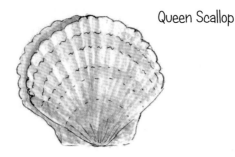

Banded Wedge Shell

Bivalves

– are aquatic molluscs, they live in a shell consisting of two halves hinged together and live on the seabed in mud and sand. When the animal dies, the shells rise to the surface of the sea to be washed up on the shore. They arrive on the beach, sometimes intact with both shells still attached, sometimes as individual ones where they have been broken apart by the waves.

Common Otter Shell

Cockle

Thin Tellin

Mussel

Oyster

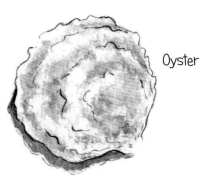

52

Gastropod Molluscs – include sea snails and sea slugs. They move using a large muscular foot. They have sensory organs on their tentacles. They often have a single asymmetrical spiral shell. They live mainly on rocky sea beds and shores under seaweed

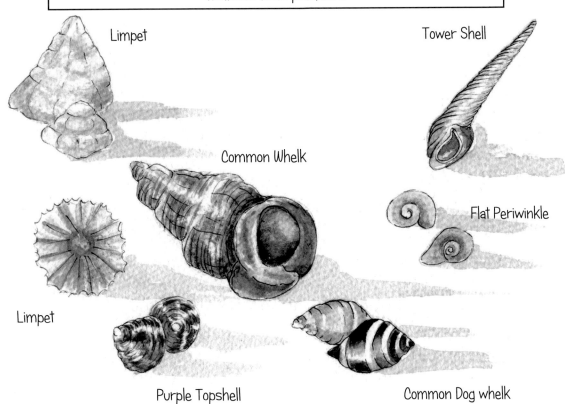

Limpet

Tower Shell

Common Whelk

Flat Periwinkle

Limpet

Purple Topshell

Common Dog whelk

Shell Candles

You will need

6 x wax tea light candles

a range of bivalve shell halves, rinsed and dried

small saucepan and heatproof bowl

pair of tongs; aluminium foil

baking tray

Note

Melted wax is very hot, please take care and wear protection while making shell candles.

DO NOT MELT THE WAX IN A MICROWAVE

How to make

Fill the saucepan with water and bring to the boil over a hob. Turn heat to lowest setting and sit the bowl over the pan. Sit one candle at a time, metal side down in the bowl until melted. Meanwhile, cover the baking tray with foil and set the shells open side up. Using tongs and oven gloves, carefully remove the candles, when ready, to the tray next to the shells. Carefully remove the wick with the metal disk using the tongs or tweezers and place in a shell. Pour the wax into the shell keeping the wick taper above the wax line. Leave to cool. Repeat with the other shells.

Baked spider crab as cooked in Spain

Created by Mitch Tonks - The Seahorse and Rockfish Restaurants

If you can, buy spider crab meat only as it's time consuming to pick. It can be made equally as successfully with meat from the more common brown crab. I like to serve this in the shell as the final grilling heats the shell and you get some wonderful aromas from it. If you have no shells a small gratin dish or scallop shell works fine.

You will need: serves 2

- 150g white spider crab meat
- 60g brown meat
- 8 cherry tomatoes quartered
- ½ clove garlic crushed to a paste
- 2 tablespoons finely chopped leeks

- 2 tablespoons finely chopped celery
- splash brandy
- splash of sherry
- 50ml double cream

- a few tarragon leaves
- teaspoon finely chopped parsley
- handful fine breadcrumbs
- knob of butter
- olive oil & salt and pepper

To Make

Add a little olive oil to a pan and soften the leeks, tomatoes, garlic and celery. Add the sherry and boil off, then add the brandy. Stir in the brown crabmeat and tarragon then the cream, taste and season then take off the heat and stir in the white meat. Pour into your dish or the crab shell then sprinkle the top with breadcrumbs and a small knob of butter then brown under the grill, sprinkle with the parsley and serve with a lemon wedge and spoon.

© Mitch Tonks www.mitchtonks.co.uk

Torquay - Meadfoot Beach

Parking - Free road parking along the beach road and on road adjacent to Meadfoot Green; Kilmorie long stay pay and display TQ1 2HX next to the beach; Anstey's Cove TQ1 2QP

Type of beach and access - Sand and pebble beach with a promenade and easy access to the beach via slipway or steps.

Cafes - Popular cafe (seasonal April – October)

Toilets - Next to the cafe. with disabled facilities

Lifeguards - The beach is supervised during July and August. check RNLI website for details. and Life buoys are available all year round.

Dogs allowed - Yes. on the North Eastern part of the beach

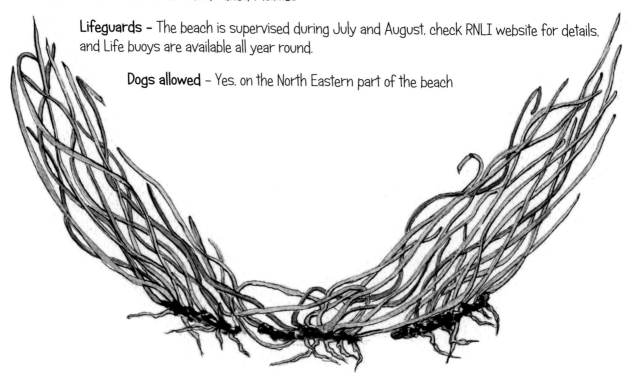

Meadfoot beach sits beneath commanding cliffs, boasting breathtaking views of Thatcher Rock about 275 metres from the shore. Looking closely, or with binoculars you can see the hundreds of layers of limestone which has taken millions of years to form............ Simply stunning.........

Skimming pebbles to see how far they will go and how many times they will bounce or ricochet on the surface of the water gives endless pleasure!

Did You Know..........
The world record for the number of skips is 88, and achieved by Kurt "Mountain Man" Steiner, age 48. He succeeded on September 6, 2013 at Red Bridge in the Allegheny National Forest, Pennsylvania.

Strand line Scavenger Hunt

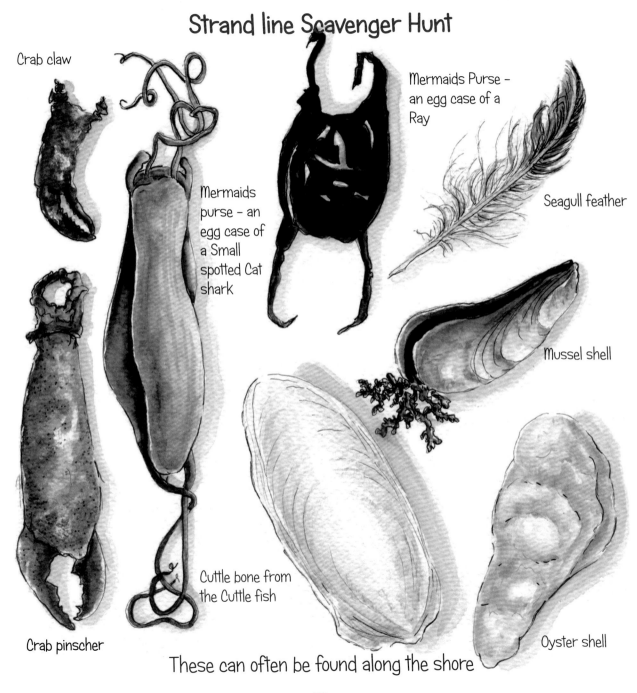

Crab claw

Mermaids purse – an egg case of a Small spotted Cat shark

Mermaids Purse – an egg case of a Ray

Seagull feather

Mussel shell

Crab pinscher

Cuttle bone from the Cuttle fish

Oyster shell

These can often be found along the shore

Leisurely Walk (about 4 miles)

Coming off the beach head up either Ilsham road with Meadfoot Green on your left, or on the Green itself, until you reach the end and join Ilsham road again. Keep on this road until you see a playing field with children's park on the right just before a bend in the road. Cross over and go through the field into Anstey's Cove car park. In the corner by the road you'll see the South West Coast Path SWCP sign which takes you through beautiful woodland known as Bishop's Walk. Follow the path keeping the coastline to your left. You will pass an area called Black Head where you can clearly see Orestone magnificently emerging from the sea. Continue walking until you come out at a junction on to Ilsham Marine Drive. Cross the road and turn left, walking along a grassy raised footpath above the road. At the end of the path cross the road (The rocky formation you see at this point is Hope's Nose and is worth going through the style to see) Continue walking down the road with the sea still on your left. And you'll soon see Thatcher Rock, with plenty of benches to take a break and admire the stunning views, or investigate a little further. As you progress down the road you will find yourself back at the beach, where you can then linger a little longer or make your way back to your car park. For a shorter walk, turn right at the junction with Ilsham Marine Drive, and follow the road which leads back to Ilsham road.

(Not to scale)

Did you know?

In many areas of this coast line fossils can easily be found, as well as pieces of extinct corals, and one of the best places to find them is at low tide at Hope's Nose on the walking route.

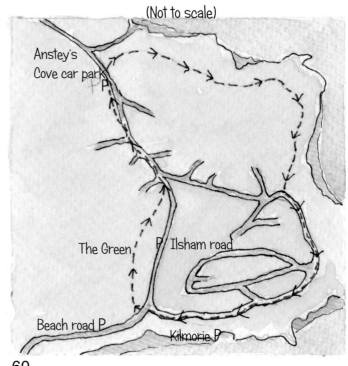

60

The uplifting view from Black Head with Orestone in the distance! Beautiful wild flowers adorn the paths like Goldilocks Aster, Nit Grass and Little Robin.

Marbled White butterfly

Painted Lady butterfly

These. possibly Maritime Pines. are planted on the hillside descending back to Meadfoot. As you pass o the walk. the view through their foliage of the coast of Torbay is breathtaking.......

Picnic Lunch

Prawn, pepper and artichoke salad

Method

Cook the pasta according to packet instructions. Allow to cool. Place the prawns in a large bowl with the peppers, artichokes, onions and olives. In a separate bowl mix the dressing ingredients together and add to the prawn mixture. Add the pasta and fold together lightly. Cover and marinate in the fridge for 3 hours turning occasionally. Transfer to a sealed food container .

Ingredients – serves 4

2 red onions, thinly sliced
125g cooked prawns
1 x 400g tin artichoke hearts
drained and quartered
150g pitted black olives
1 x jar of roasted red peppers cut
into 1 cm pieces
280g large pasta shapes

Dressing

125ml olive oil.
2 tbsp white wine vinegar.
1 crushed garlic clove
grated rind and juice of a lemon
2 teasp honey
2 tbsp fresh chives, chopped

A short distance from the shore in shallow waters grow seagrass beds; meadows of long and narrow ribbon shaped leaved grasses which are the only group of true marine flowering plants. They grow mainly on sandy sea beds and need sunlight to flourish. Seagrass grows by a rhizome root system under the seabed moving downward and horizontally along at the same time as leaves are produced vertically. The grass stabilizes the sandy bottom of the sea in a similar way that grass on land reduces soil erosion.

Seagrass helps to reduce greenhouse gases by cleaning the surrounding water, removing carbon dioxide and producing oxygen.

Due to damage partly from pollution, and partly from humans by trampling, dredging, as well as mooring and anchoring there is a decline globally at a rate of around 7%per year. The three species found in the UK are scarce and now come under the UK Bio diversity Action Plan (BAP) Priority Habitat.

The Community Seagrass Initiative (CSI) is a citizen science project led by the National Marine Aquarium and local partners in five regions of the South West from Looe in Cornwall to Ringstead in Dorset. Torbay has five main seagrass beds, two off Torquay and three off Brixham. The aim of the initiative is to provide volunteers and members of the public an opportunity to be involved with identifying vital data on seagrass beds and the presence of algae and identifying commercial fish species from images from their photo surveys on line. There are also opportunities for volunteers from the diving, kayaking and sailing communities to be involved with the project. Like the 'Sailing into Science' activity.

Seagrass beds provide a nursery habitat for a number of local species including pollack and scallops. Cuttlefish attach eggs to the seagrass stems, to keep them safe from predators, and seagrass provides a very suitable and important environment for our two rare native seahorses.

There are two species of seahorse in the UK, both can be found in Torbay: the Short Snouted Seahorse and the Spiny Seahorse (shown here). They grow to around 15cms and have the ability to vary their body colour allowing them to hide and camouflage themselves in the seagrass from predators. They cling to the seagrass which prevents them from being swept away by strong current.

As they are monogamous, when seahorses choose a partner they mate for life. They are very unusual and unique in that it is the male who carries the growing young, the female having passed on her eggs into a pouch on the stomach of the male, where after fertilisation they stay until he gives birth about three weeks later to fully formed seahorses.

Seaweed comes in all shapes and sizes and there is little to beat the colourful spectrum of a rock pool filled with shades of red, brown and green plants, almost artistically arranged for our viewing, glistening in the sunlight, a spectacular water feature.......

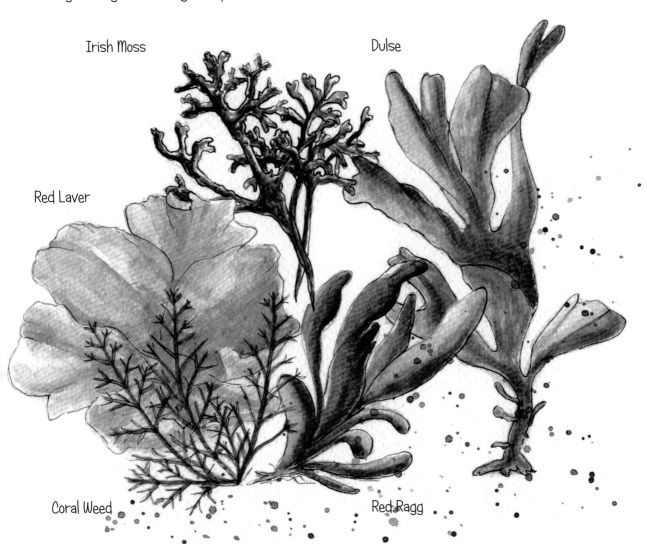

Irish Moss

Dulse

Red Laver

Coral Weed

Red Ragg

Oarweed can grow up to 2 metres long, forming 'fingers' at its tips and clings to low rocks up to 20 metres deep. Most often seen washed up on the beach as this was.

Furbellows

Oarweed

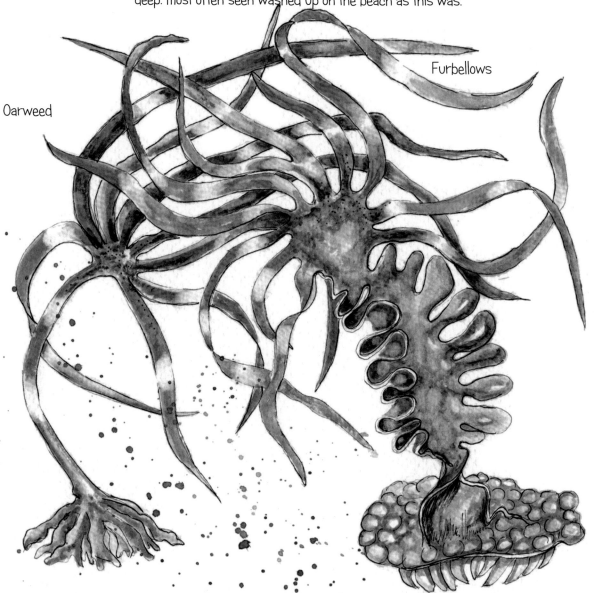

Furbellows can grow to 3 metres and has large bulbous, hedgehog like base which attaches to rocks, a flattened oar-like stripe with frilly edges at its base. Often seen on the beach.

Coastal Driftwood Ornaments

You will need

pencil . scissors

small driftwood or smooth sticks
(please don't remove driftwood from
sand dunes as it is an important
wildlife habitat)

recycled cardboard (from packaging)

craft glue

How to make

Draw a coastal design of your choice (ideas below)
on the cardboard. Cut out the shapes. Match,
where you can, the right length of driftwood or
sticks to your design, slightly overlapping the
cardboard and cut to match for the rest of your
design. When you're happy with it, glue the
driftwood to the card and use a bit of salvaged
cork or small piece of driftwood for the eyes if
wanted. Leave overnight to dry.

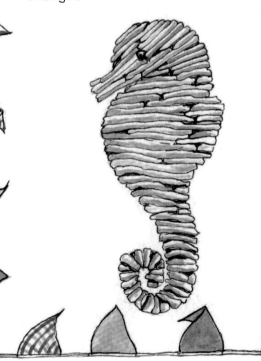

Pan fried turbot fillet with a lemon butter and chervil sauce

Created by Oliver Stacey, No 7 Fish Bistro, Torquay

Ingredients: serves 2

2 x 200-250g turbot fillet (brill or hake could be used as an alternative.)

500ml fish stock (any left over can be frozen for next time); 200g clarified salted butter

1tbsp lemon juice; 100ml white wine

40g unsalted butter cut into small cubes covered with water and refrigerated for minimum 2-3 hours or overnight.

small handful of chervil or dill, stalks removed and finely chopped; sea salt and black pepper.

Method.

Bring the fish stock to the boil and simmer until reduced by two thirds. This can be done in advance then refrigerated. Brush a non stick frying pan with some of the clarified butter and place on high heat. As this heats, season the fish with sea salt and black pepper as desired. Once the pan begins to smoke, carefully place the fish flesh side down into the pan. Cook for 2-3 minutes or until lightly coloured. Remove the fish from the pan and place skin side down onto a baking tray brushed with clarified butter. Place the fish into a pre heated oven (200 deg C) for 7-8 minutes or until hot at the thickest part of the fillet. You can test this with the the thin end of a teaspoon or a skewer. While the fish is cooking, add: 3 tbsp of reduced fish stock into a sauce pan, 1 tablespoon of lemon juice, white wine and the cold butter; whisk over a high heat until thickened. Season to taste then the add chervil/dill and remove from the heat. Place the fish under a high grill for 20-30 seconds then plate, pouring the sauce over the fish.

Note: if sauce becomes too thick, add a dash more of the reduced fish stock or white wine.

www.no7-fish.com

Teignmouth Town Beach

Parking – Teign Street car park TQ14 8EL pay and display: The Point car park TQ14 8SY pay and display: Brunswick Street car park TQ14 8AF pay and display, plus street parking

Type of beach and access – Sandy beach, good access from the road including disabled access

Cafes – A range of local cafes, shops and restaurants

Toilets – toilets with disabled access along the seafront and in town

Lifeguards – Yes, check RNLI website for details

Dogs allowed – Yes out of season, but allowed all year on Back Beach

The magnificent Teignmouth Grand Pier stands proudly and indeed with grandeur! Built in 1865 it has seen much history and could. I'm sure. tell many a sea faring tale ....

So nostalgic to wonder along the promenade and see a lighthouse built over a hundred years ago still providing a life saving purpose today..........

The small, Grade 11 listed lighthouse on the 'Den' was completed in 1845 and is 28 feet tall with 2 foot thick walls. Although small in size it is an important navigational aid maintained by the Harbour Master today. It displays a red light and is visible for approx 6 miles. allowing vessels a safe passage across the sand bars at the mouth of the River Teign and the safety of the harbour.

The beach huts on Back Beach offer an abundance of design skills. shapes. sizes and colours. inviting all who pass to dream of long summer days!

Hopscotch

Mark a hopscotch design in the sand using a pebble, stick or shell. Check the squares are large enough to fit one foot.

To play the game throw a flat stone or shell to land on the first square. It must land inside the square, not touching the edge. If it doesn't land within the lines, you lose your turn and the stone is passed to the next person. If you do get it though, go on to the next step.

Hop through the squares, missing out the one you have your pebble on. Each square takes one foot. You can only have one foot on the ground at a time, *unless* there are two number squares right next to each other, when you can put both feet down at the same time, one in each square. Your feet must always stay inside the square(s); if you hop on the wrong square, step on a line, or step out of the square, you lose your turn. When you get to square 10, turn (still on one foot) and in reverse order, 10 –1, hop your way back. When you get to square 2 lean down and pick up your pebble from square 1, still on one foot! Then, skip over that square to finish the round.

If you completed the course with your pebble on square one, throw it again onto square two and repeat the moves. The aim is to complete the course with the pebble on each square. The first person to do this wins the game!

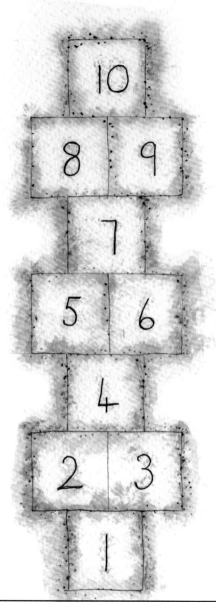

Did You Know..............
The 'game' of Hopscotch began during the early Roman Empire in ancient Britain and was used as a training exercise for the military. The hopscotch courts were over 90 metres long and would certainly have tested soldiers military strength and speed!

Leisurely Walk (about 1.5 miles)

Starting at the lighthouse, on the seafront, walk along the promenade with the sea on your right, and the Grand Pier clearly in view. On your left, the Den is a perfect picnic area with the Teignmouth Pavilions just beyond the bowling green. Continue along the promenade until Regent street. Cross over into the street and a short distance along you'll see Triangle Place (also known as the Triangle) to your left. Take a wonder around the listed two tier polished granite fountain and local interesting independent shops, before returning to the main road and continuing along Wellington Street and Bank Street until you come to a cross road. Turn left into Somerset Place and continue, crossing the road at George street and into Northumberland Place, forming the centre of the 'Teignmouth River Beach Art's Quarters' where a number of galleries, shops, cafes, pubs and restaurants add a vibrant and unique atmosphere. (See TAAG note below) Continue towards the seafront down Powderham Terrace to see the RNLI shop and boathouse. Here turn right to stroll along Back Beach, a small sandy harbour, on the estuary and enjoy the brightly coloured, individually designed beach huts and range of working boats. As you leave the beach you'll find yourself back at the lighthouse where you started.

Teignmouth Arts Action Group (TAAG) has been at the forefront of the Art scene since 2007 and has been instrumental in removing barriers and boundaries to enable Teignmouth to become an Arts town. The Arts and Community Centre is home to the TRAIL (the popular sculpture trail on Teignmouth seafront) It provides a space for Voluntary Organisations and Societies, multi cultural and poetry festivals, and is host for the Biennial International Art Exhibition. It is a workshop venue for book clubs, art workshops, camera club, jazz club, language teaching, mosaics, printmaking and philosophy while hosting over 30 art exhibitions a year for local artists

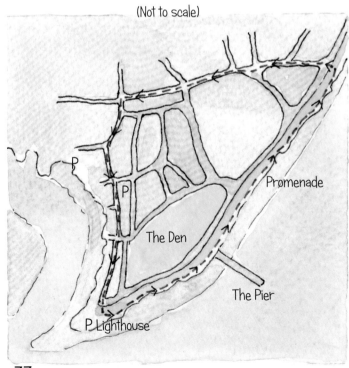

(Not to scale)

Promenade

The Den

The Pier

P Lighthouse

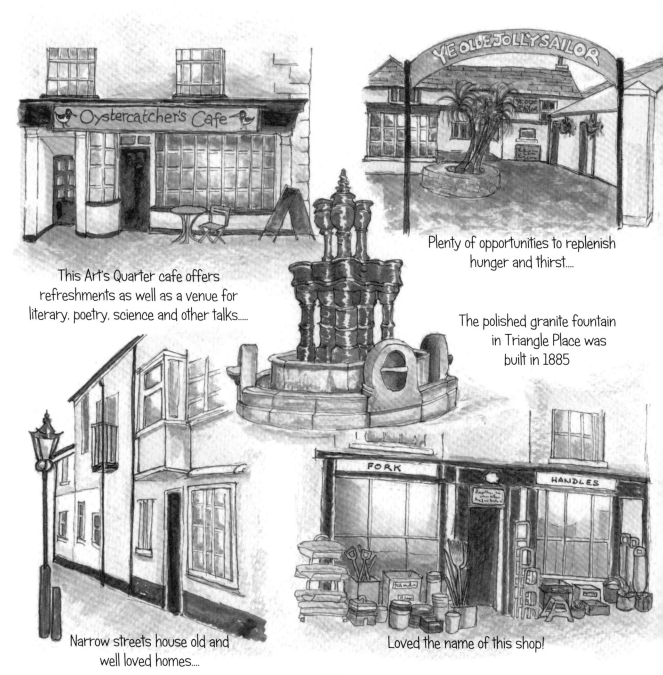

Oystercatcher's Cafe

This Art's Quarter cafe offers refreshments as well as a venue for literary, poetry, science and other talks.....

Plenty of opportunities to replenish hunger and thirst....

The polished granite fountain in Triangle Place was built in 1885

Narrow streets house old and well loved homes....

Loved the name of this shop!

78

Carnival time in Teignmouth!

The Owl and the Pussy Cat

MOLLOYS

79

Picnic Lunch

Butternut squash and Feta Feast!

Ingredients - serves 4

1 medium butternut squash
paprika and olive oil
packet of rocket
pack of Greek feta cheese
handful of black olives
2 tbsp pumpkin seeds
handful of fresh basil or parsley
herbs, chopped

Method

Peel and slice or dice the butternut squash into bite size pieces. Place on a baking tray, drizzle and toss in 2 tbsp olive oil, then sprinkle 1 teasp paprika over the squash and bake in the oven for about 30 minutes on 200C, 400F, gas mark 6. Take out and allow to cool. Place the squash and it's juices in a large bowl with all the other ingredients, except the pumpkin seeds and gently mix together until combined. Place in a sealed container and scatter the pumpkin seeds over to complete the dish.

Teignmouth Arts and Community Centre in Northumberland Place – attracting over 30,000 visitors a year to it's resource hub within the community as well as it's wide reaching art exhibitions. Run by volunteers it is open daily from 10.00 am to 5.00 pm. Well worth a visit at any time of the year!

Teignmouth Recycled Art In Landscape

TRAIL is a voluntary artist led organisation raising awareness of environmental issues through art and education. Established since 2005. TRAIL continues to give professional artists. schools. community groups and amateur artists the opportunity to create and exhibit large scale art works for an outdoor environment. During the summer the promenade is awash with stunning. distinctive. artwork designs made from re-cycled materials!

'Digitally Re - mastered Fish' A cleverly designed and created piece of artwork using CD's and DVD's by Amy McCarthy and Sam Lock.

'Teignmouth Tin Man and His Dog' made distinctively from old tins! Created by Mike and Kerry Leaman

Check the TRAIL website for current events. issues and new findings on an environmental. recycled and education theme. that help to improve the local environment and awareness.

'Give Bees a Chance'

By Michelle Greenwood-Brown and Rose Bailey

A beautifully created mosaic artwork reminding us of the plight of bees... made from mosaic tiles and pieces, recycled china teapots and earthenware pots. Teapot lids have been used for the centre of the flowers.....

A Pin Wheel for the Breeze!

You will need

A4 paper; pencil; scissors; hole punch; bradawl; paper straws; paper pin fasteners

How to make

Fold one corner of the paper to make a triangle and cut along the edge. Fold the triangle again in half, then unfold. Cut down 2/3 of each crease and punch one hole on all four of the flaps (same side for each flap) Make a small hole in the middle of the paper, then make one about 1cm down from one end of the straw. Gently pull the four corners with holes into the middle of the paper then push the paper fastener through both the paper and straw, opening it out to secure.

Oysters a la Florentine with a panko and parmesan crust

Created by Christiane Cook

Ingredients: serves 4

12 medium sized fresh oysters – preferably wild

1 bag of washed baby spinach

1 tbsp crème fraiche; 1 tsp freshly grated nutmeg

2 oz plain flour; 350 ml whole milk (heated)

2 oz gruyere cheese - grated

1-2 tbsp panko breadcrumbs

1-2 tbsp freshly grated parmesan

Salt & Pepper; 2 oz unsalted butter

Method

Firstly, wilt down the spinach in a large saucepan. Drain into a colander and squeeze out any liquid. Return to a bowl, stir in the crème fraiche and season with salt and pepper. Add the grated nutmeg and mix well – set aside. Make up the mornay sauce; Melt the butter over a low heat. Gradually add the flour and stir thoroughly off the heat for a couple of minutes making sure to "cook out" the flour. Return the pan to the heat and slowly add the milk, a little at a time, until it is all incorporated and you have a smooth, thick sauce. Stir in the grated cheese and set aside. In a small bowl mix together the panko breadcrumbs, grated parmesan and season. Assemble the oysters; carefully open each oyster making sure not to leave any shell in the oyster, loosen each one from its shell and drain well – keeping it in the shell. Spoon 1 tbsp spinach on top of each oyster. Next, spoon 1 tbsp mornay sauce on top, making sure to cover the spinach completely. Finally, sprinkle a handful of the panko breadcrumb and parmesan mixture over the top. Pre heat your grill until hot and place the oysters under the grill on a metal tray for approximately 5-6 minutes. You should see the sauce just beginning to bubble and the breadcrumbs browning slightly. Remove from the grill and serve at once with Jersey Royal potatoes and a green salad.

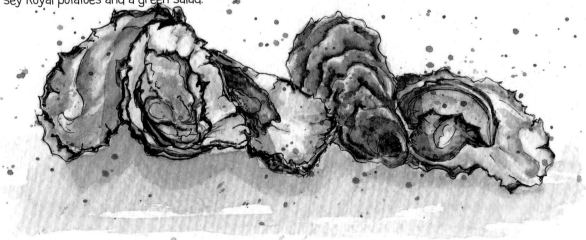

Dawlish Warren

Parking – There are 2 car parks, both pay and display at Beach Walk. EX7 0NF. Outer Car Park – The entrance is on the right at the roundabout before the tunnel; Inner Car Park – is on the other side of the tunnel nearer the beach

Type of beach and access – 1.5 miles of sandy beach with plenty of sand dunes. Easy access for all

Cafes – A range of cafes for refreshments

Toilets – with disabled access near the cafes

Lifeguards – Yes – From July – September, check RNLI website for details

Dogs allowed – Yes via access at groyne 3 – 9 during April to September. and from 1 –9 the rest of the year

The beach huts ready and waiting to offer a unique experience at the edge of the beach at Dawlish Warren

The groynes work endlessly to manage the incoming tide. keeping a check on erosion and drifting.......... no small task!

The stories these could tell.......worn by age and sea. they still look magnificent!

Coming up from the beach the sand dunes beckon me forwards, their grasses whispering in the gentle breeze......

The National Nature Reserve paths meander through the sand dunes and grasses, and provide a beautifully quiet, peaceful backdrop to the sounds of birds and wildlife in abundance, butterfly and insect activity mesmerising my senses..........

Picnic Lunch

Pumpkin Soup with fresh crusty bread!

Ingredients – serves 4

2 tbsp olive oil
1 medium onion
600g pumpkin (or squash) diced
1 teasp paprika
3 tbsp tomato puree
85g split red lentils
900ml vegetable stock (using a stock cube)
fresh crusty bread of your choice

Method

Add the oil and onions to a large pan and cook until soft. Introduce the pumpkin (or squash) along with all other soup ingredients and bring to the boil gently stirring occasionally. Cover the pot and simmer for 25/30 minutes until cooked. Use a hand held blender to puree the soup and transfer to a flask or other food container. Serve with fresh crusty bread

Leisurely Walk (about 3 miles)

Starting at the inner car park head towards the reserve and dunes following the path, keeping the golf course on your left. There is a choice of paths but all lead in the same direction. You will pass the Visitor Centre, open in the season and well worth stopping for a browse. Continue through kissing gates to a narrower path meandering through the dunes. This will bring you to an area called the Bight. (Just before here if you have dogs follow the signs which cut across towards the beach area avoiding the sensitive nature reserve at Warren Point. Further signs lead you back via the beach between groynes 9 and 3 or continue your walk on the dunes and grasses.) At the Bight, bear right on the sandy beach. After a short distance you can either stay on the beach (if the tide allows) or when you see a post with its top painted red, you can return to the dunes paths. Keep following the path or beach until you return to the start of your walk near the car park.

In late March to May you can see the Sand or Warren Crocus, rarely found anywhere other than Dawlish Warren. They are pale purple with purple veins and have 6 pointed petals and are only 12mm across!

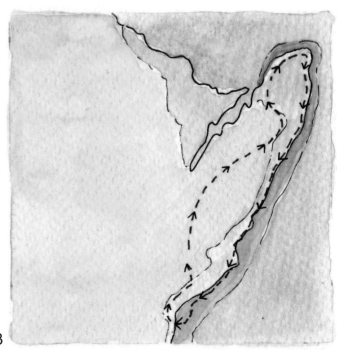

Such a variety of grasses......

Marram grass

Sea couch grass

Sand sedge

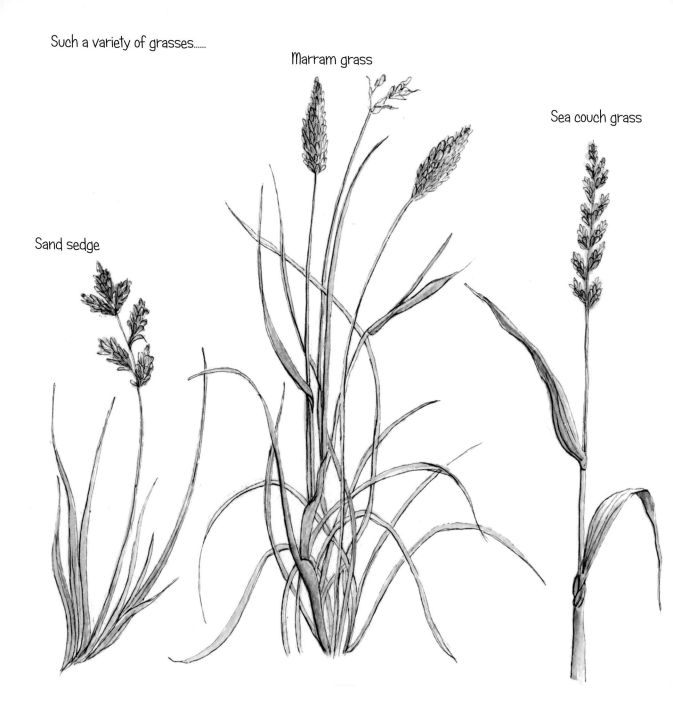

Oystercatcher

Found along the estuary and shoreline, they are easy to recognise with striking black and white plumage. They are a spectacle in flight. They are wading birds, and have reddish-pink legs. Their bills are long and orange-red. Unlike their name suggests they rarely feed on oysters, preferring other bivalves like cockles and mussels and their strong bills are perfectly suited to prying open these molluscs. They have an unmistakable loud 'peep-ing' call which they often let you hear way before you see them!

Did you know?

You can age a cockle shell by the dark bands which run around the outside of the shell across the prominent ribs. Cockles usually live for 2 - 4 years some much longer.

95

Oystercatcher feather and Eggs

The nest of the oystercatcher is not as you'd expect. rather they lay their eggs in a scrape in the ground which both the male and female take turns to incubate.

The Bar - Tailed Godwit

Is another long billed wading bird who either spends the winters here on sandy shores and estuaries or passes through en route to warmer climes, originating from as far away as Siberia and Alaska. They forage in mud flats or marshes for insects, shrimps, shellfish, snails and worms.

Avocet

This stunningly elegant black and white wader is a winter visitor to the shoreline and estuary. They have an unmistakable up curved bill which they use in a sideways sweep in the water to capture small shrimps and worms.

Curlew

A popular and easily recognised wading bird. It's gentle down turned, long purpose built bill enables it to efficiently seek out and eat invertebrates, ragworms, worms and small crabs on the muddy estuary and shoreline during the winter months spent in coastal areas. The summer months being spent in meadows, fields and marshes, the perfect breeding grounds.

Look out for these footprints as you explore the beach and sand dunes....

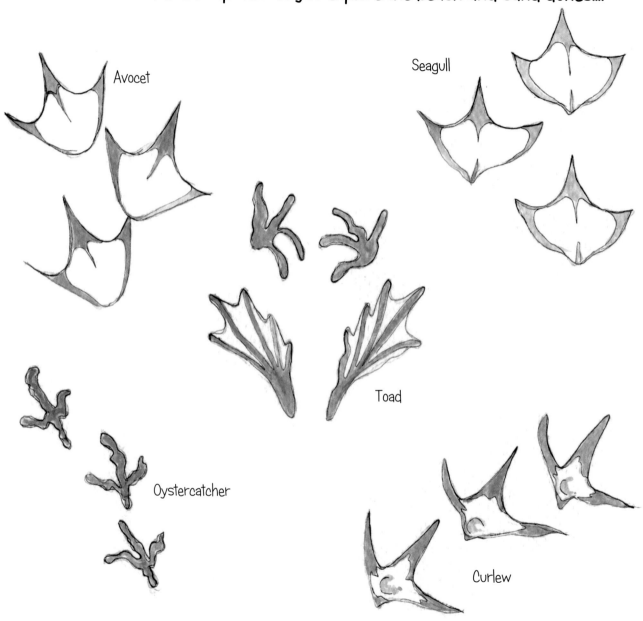

Avocet

Seagull

Toad

Oystercatcher

Curlew

Cockles and Mussels

You will need

4 small pieces of driftwood or sticks
(please don't remove driftwood from sand dunes as
it is an important wildlife habitat)
5 cockle and 5 mussel shells (or other shells)
small amount of string or thread

How to make

Assemble the driftwood as shown and tie the overlaps
of wood with short pieces of string or thread, crossing
over and secure with a knot.

2 players use either cockle or mussel shells to play the
equivalent of Naught's and Crosses! A player must get
a line of 3 shells the same to win.

Seafood linguine topped with seared red mullet

Created by Ian Dodd, the Smugglers Inn, Dawlish

You will need – serves 4

1 white onion (fine diced); 1 ½ stalks of celery (fine diced); ½ leek (fine diced)

150ml white wine; 100ml vegetable stock (made with a stock cube)

100ml fish stock (made with a stock cube); juice of 1 lemon; 500ml double cream; 250ml ready made béchamel

500gm seafood mix (e.g. mussels, cockles, prawns, scallops, octopus; squid – liquid drained)

1 or 2 cod fillet (chopped); tsp. of 50/50 white/brown crabmeat (optional) tblsp dill (chopped)

4 red mullet fillets; salt and pepper; 280gm dry linguine pasta or 200gm fresh linguine pasta

seasoned boiling water with a splash of oil; 1 white baguette to serve

Method:

Cook the linguine in the oiled and seasoned boiling water, as per packet instructions, then cool down for later. Sweat off the onion, leek and celery. Add the white wine, lemon juice, vegetable and fish stock then whisk to combine. Add cream and béchamel and bring to the boil checking sauce consistency. Add the seafood mix and cod, then simmer. Once fish is cooked add the crab and dill and stir. Sear the Red mullet fillets for 4 minutes skin side down, then flip and cook for a further 1 minute. Add the cooked linguine to the seafood mix, season to taste. Serve topped with the red mullet and a crusty white baguette.

www.thesmugglersinn.net

Exmouth

Parking – Queens Echelon EX8 2AY and Foxholes Hill EX8 2DG both on the seafront, both pay and display.

Type of beach and access – About 2 miles of sandy beach with easy access via level access, slipway and steps with a promenade.

Cafes – Plenty of cafes, shops and restaurants

Toilets – On the seafront

Lifeguards – Yes, from July – September, check RNLI website for details

Dogs allowed – welcome all year on parts of the beach, clear signs

Orcombe point from Maer beach. Its taken millions of years to create the incredible rock formations..........
This is the start of the Jurassic coast!

A wonderful sight as horses and riders take to Maer beach!

Exmouth offers such a wonderful expanse of beach and parking. There's room for everyone!

Around Orcombe Point, walking towards Sandy Bay..... I love the flat topped ripple marks on the sand, only present until the next tide when the design will change again!

No matter what time of year and what type of weather, the beach will always be a place to let imaginations explore endless possibilities, whether treasure hunting, digging for gold or designing and building a magnificent castle!

To stroll along the beach, hear waves gently rolling in, feel the sand between our toes and soak up the atmosphere of freedom, all to the sound of seabirds is a truly memorable day out.

How lovely to know the beach is clean too......

Everyone can do a bit to help keep our beaches clean. Always take rubbish home or find a bin for it. Check out local websites to see when Community Beach Cleans are being held and join one!

There is a great sense of satisfaction knowing, as part of a community, you have been part of a group helping to remove plastic, and other insoluble waste from our coastlines and seas................

Picnic Lunch

Devon Ploughmans with Chilli jam

Ingredients – serves 4

180g red chillies, de-seeded and roughly chopped
180g red peppers, de-seeded and roughly chopped
2cm piece of root ginger
400ml cider vinegar
1kg jam sugar
local Devon cheese of your choice
freshly baked french stick
green salad

Method

Blitz the chillies, peppers and ginger in a food processor, blender or hand held blender. Place in a large saucepan together with the cider vinegar and jam sugar (which includes pectin) Simmer on a rolling boil for 15 minutes. Take the pan off the heat and allow to cool. As it does it will become the consistency of jam. Ladle the jam into sterilised jars, top with lids and label.

Serve with the bread, cheese and salad.

Tip – Sterilise three or four clean small jars and their lids in the oven for 15 minutes at 140C/275F/gas mark 1 before you start your jam, then they're ready to fill.

Leisurely Walk (about 2.5 miles)

Starting at the car parks, head east along the promenade with the sea on your right until you reach the end of the beach and will see notices and plaques explaining about the Jurassic coast. On your left will be a foot path heading upwards in a zig zag manner. Follow this path to the top and bear right. This will take you through an easy to follow route to the Highland of Orcombe and on to Orcombe point. Here is where you can see the Geoneedle and enjoy amazing views across Exmouth over to Starcross and Dawlish. Continue along the the well defined path following signs for Sandy Bay, through the holiday park and cafe until you reach the beach. Once on the sand make your return journey across the bay, rounding Orcombe point and returning along Maer beach.

Please Note
As this walk involves crossing the beach.......

Please check tide times before starting this walk. If the tides are high you will have to re arrange to do the walk another time. or return from Sandy Bay retracing your steps.

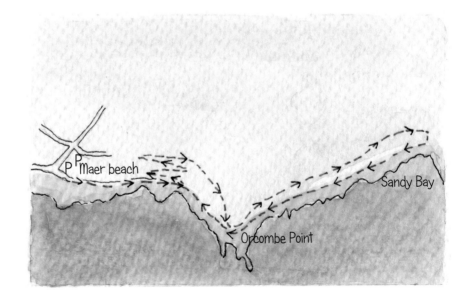

As you walk along the paths, plenty of signs lead you to the right destination, wherever you are heading............

THE NATIONAL TRUST
HIGH LAND OF ORCOMBE

COAST PATH
GEONEEDLE 2/3m
EXMOUTH 2⅔m.

COAST PATH
BUDLEIGH
SALTERTON

SANDY
BAY

INCREDIBLE

The South West Coast Path runs through Orcombe Point and the Jurassic Coast. This National Trail is over 1,000km (630 miles) long, from Minehead in north Somerset to Poole Harbour in Dorset

ORCOMBE

Coast Path
Exmouth

Orcombe Point
& Geoneedle

COAST PATH
VIA RODNEY POINT

The Geoneedle at Orcombe Point

Commemorates the opening of the World Heritage Site in 2002 and is made up from the various rock types which have formed over the last approx. 180 million years! It marks the beginning of the Jurassic Coast which follows 96 miles of coastal path to Swanage in Dorset.............I may not walk that all today!

There is a small 'Jurassic coast hopscotch' beside it made up from stones of the different ages

Around Orcombe Point

A flurry of white blossom clouds in spring turns to sloe berries in the autumn.....

The Solitary Bee - often makes tunnels next to paths, lay their eggs and leave food for their young. They don't sting and so are safe.

The Stonechat - is about the size of a robin and has an unmistakable call, a sharp sound like two stones being clapped together!

The Bloody Nosed Beetle cannot fly and so is often seen wondering across paths. It has a strange way to defend itself, by spraying an unpleasant red liquid from it's mouth to deter predators!

Fragrant yellow Gorse flowers in spring hide the thorny stems which help protect nest's of the Stonechat and other birds as well as providing food and shelter for a range of insects

Exmouth Lifeboat Station

Situated at the eastern end of Queen's Drive. it was opened in 2009. but the first life boat was positioned here in 1803. Today the station houses a Shannon Class vessel. an all weather lifeboat with a length of 13.6m and max speed of 25 knots able to accommodate 6 crew. and a D Class inflatable lifeboat for shallow water taking 2-3 crew.

The station provides opportunities to watch the Shannon lifeboat exercises as well as open days. Free tours of the Lifeboat Station are provided by volunteers at specific times and certainly well worth being part of........

A fun 'Face in the Hole Board' gives everyone a chance to feel like a crew member!

Make and Fly a Kite

You will need

A4 piece of paper; crayons or paints to decorate
stapler and hole punch
ball of string, jute or cotton thread

How to make

Decorate one side of the paper with patterns or shapes. Fold the paper in half, as shown. Make a mark about 5 cms in from one end of the folded edge, and a further mark about 2cms down from the first mark. Bend the top front corner towards the crease and repeat with the back layer, in the opposite direction (don't fold or crease them) Staple in place. Make a hole on the second mark. Thread the string through and tie it off with a knot tightly.

Add some ribbons!

Fly your kite!

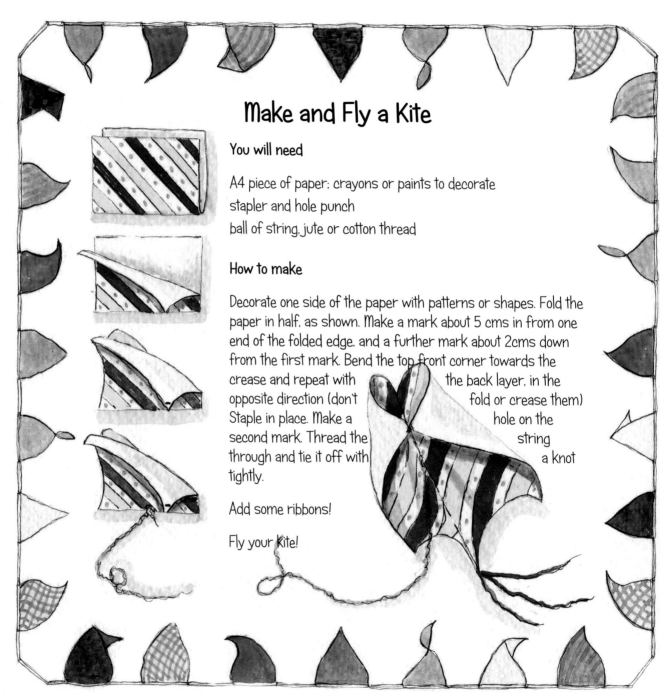

Across the sand dunes and on to the beach ....Let's go fly a kite!

Mussel and sea spinach tart with blood orange and watercress salad and saffron mayonnaise

Created by Nigel Wright and Kerry Dow, Saveur, Exmouth

Sea spinach can be found on various coastlines, common along estuaries and pebble shorelines, it has an earthy taste and robust texture. As with any foraging please pick sensibly and ensure you know what you are picking. Alternatively you can use baby spinach.

For the pastry: serves 6
Plain flour 225g; Salt 1/2 tsp
Chilled butter 65g cut into pieces
Chilled lard 65g cut into pieces; Cold water 1-2 tbsp;

Filling
300g mussel meat; 6 eggs; 600ml double cream
80g blanched and squeezed sea spinach
240g Quickes Red Leicester cheese grated
1tbsp chopped tarragon; 2tbsp chopped chive
Salt and pepper

Salad
1 bunch watercress; 2 blood oranges
segmented and lightly chopped (reserve juice
from remains for dressing); 20g toasted
pumpkin seeds; 30ml blood orange juice from
above; 30ml extra virgin rapeseed oil; Pinch
sugar; Season to taste

Saffron mayonnaise
1/2 teaspoon saffron soaked in tsp hot water
60g mayonnaise
1tsp lemon juice
1/2tsp Dijon mustard

Method

For the pastry

Sieve the salt and flour into a large mixing bowl or food processor then add the lard and butter and work together until you have the consistency of fine breadcrumbs. With a pallet knife gradually stir in the water until the mixture comes together as a ball. Place the ball on a lightly floured surface and knead until smooth. Pre heat oven to 220C/gas 7. Roll out the pastry and use to line 6 flan tins lightly greased (10cm loose based). Chill for 30 minutes then line pastry cases with baking paper and baking beans and bake for 15 -18 minutes until base cooked. Remove paper and beans and brush each case with egg wash then bake for a further 3 minutes. Once done remove from oven and reset temperature to 160C/gas 3.

For the mayonnaise

Soak saffron in hot water for 5 minutes then whisk all ingredients (including saffron water) into mayonnaise. check for seasoning and refrigerate until ready to use.

To make filling

Beat eggs, herbs and cream lightly in a bowl and season with salt and pepper. Arrange spinach (thoroughly squeezed to remove excess water) mussels and cheese evenly into tart cases and then pour over egg mixture ensuring even distribution of herbs. Bake for 20-25 minutes until custard is set and pastry is golden brown.

For the salad

Place watercress, blood orange, and pumpkin seeds in bowl. Mix blood orange juice, seasoning and oil vigorously in jar and then dress salad.

Serve the tarts warm with dressed salad and mayonnaise.

www.saveursrestaurant.com

Useful Websites

National Trust www.nationaltrust.org.uk
Wembury Marine Centre www.wemburymarinecentre.org
Devon Wildlife Trust www.devonwildlifetrust.org
Slapton Ley Field Studies Council www.field-studies-council.org
Exercise Tiger Memorial www.exercisetigermemorial.co.uk
RSPB www.rspb.org.uk
Tide Times www.tidetimes.org.uk
Marine Conservation Society www.mcsuk.org
British Sea Fishing www.britishseafishing.co.uk
Fishcombe Eco Mooring www.countryside-trust.org.uk
Community Seagrass Initiative www.csi-seagrass.co.uk
Seahorse Trust www.theseahorsetrust.org
TAAG Teignmouth Arts & Community Centre www.teignmoutharts.org
Teignmouth Recycled Art In Landscape. TRAIL www.trailart.co.uk
Dawlish Warren Nature Reserve www.devonwildlifetrust.org
The Jurassic Coast World Heritage Site www.jurassiccoast.org
Exmouth RNLI lifeboat station www.exmouthlifeboat.org.uk
Beach Clean - Surfers against Sewage www.sas.org.uk
Butterfly Conservation www.butterfly-conservation.org

Acknowledgements

The restaurant recipes reproduced here are printed with the kind permission of:

Pan fried scallops, smoked bacon and spinach by Nick & Anita Hutchings of Britannia at the Beach www.britanniaatthebeach.co.uk

Thai fish cakes by South Devon Chilli Farm www.southdevonchillifarm.co.uk

Baked spider crab as cooked in Spain by Mitch Tonks of Seahorse and Rockfish Restaurants www.mitchtonks.co.uk

Pan fried turbot fillet, lemon butter, chervil sauce by Oliver Stacey of No 7 Fish Restaurant www.no7-fish.com

Oysters a la florentine with a panko and parmesan crust by Christiane Cook

Seafood linguine topped with seared red mullet by Ian Dodd of The Smugglers Inn www.thesmugglersinn.net

Mussel and sea spinach tart with blood orange and watercress salad, saffron mayonnaise by Nigel Wright and Kerry Dow of Saveur Restaurant www.saveursrestaurant.com

I would like to thank the following for sharing their knowledge and professional help:

Sarah Goble – National Trust: Use of recognised walks and branded signs, courtesy of National Trust www.nationaltrust.org.uk

Andy Pratt – Field Studies Council: Use of Ley walks and signs, courtesy of Field Studies Council www.field-studies-council.org

Alex Turner – South West Coast Path

Dan Smith – Devon Wildlife Trust: Use of the Trusts Seashore Code, courtesy of Devon Wildlife Trust www.devonwildlifetrust.org

Mark Parry – Community Seagrass Initiative. Use of the CSI logo courtesy of Community Seagrass Initiative www.csi-seagrass.co.uk

Amy McCarthy – TRAIL Art Teignmouth: Artwork by local artists, courtesy of TRAIL www.trailart.co.uk

Open Street Map – www.openstreetmap.org

Thank you to friends who have helped and supported me along the way,
especially Frecks, Tony, Ann, Pat, Gez and Yvonne

And finally to my family – for all their love and support and for always being there for me.
To my husband John for his non-wavering support, encouragement, and tolerance, while creating this book, as well as sharing his amazing technical skills!

To my children – Thank you for your contributions to the picnic recipes, and your faith in me.

I got there!